THE POISON OF PORN

THE POISON OF PORN

Helping young men navigate safely away from pornography

Frank R. Shivers

Printed in partnership with Iron Stream Media
Birmingham, Alabama

Copyright 2020 by
Frank Shivers Evangelistic Association
All rights reserved
Printed in the United States of America

Unless otherwise noted, Scripture quotations are from
The Holy Bible *King James Version*

Library of Congress Cataloging-in-Publication Data

Shivers, Frank R., 1949-
The Poison of Porn / Frank Shivers
ISBN 978-1-878127-39-6

Library of Congress Control Number:
2019905605

For Information:
Frank Shivers Evangelistic Association
P. O. Box 9991
Columbia, South Carolina 29290
www.frankshivers.com

Presented to

_____

By

_____

Date

_____

All provident Lord, place Your holy fear as a guard before my eyes so they may not look lustfully; before my ears so that they may not delight in hearing evil words; before my mouth so that it may not speak any falsehoods; before my heart so that it may not think evil; before my hands so that they may not do injustice; before my feet, that they may not walk in the paths of injustice; but so direct them, that they may always be according to all Your commandments. Have mercy upon Your Creatures and upon me, a great sinner, I pray in the Name of Christ. Amen.

~ (St.) Nersess the Gracious, 12th century

The greatest threat to the cause of Christ is pervasive sexuality and pornography.[1]

~ Josh McDowell

The battle of life as a whole will probably not rise above the sex battle. Lose the sex battle, and defeat spreads into every portion of your being. Win it, and all of life is lifted by that victory.[2]

~ E. Stanley Jones (20th century missionary and theologian)

Man loves his own ruin. The cup of pleasure is so sweet that though he knows it will poison him—yet he must drink it. And the harlot is so lovely, that though he understands that her ways lead down to Hell—yet like a bullock he follows to the slaughter until the dart goes through his liver! Man is fascinated and bewitched by sin.[3]

~ C. H. Spurgeon

Pornography is the idea that sex can be divorced from love, from morality, from responsibility, from lifetime commitment—that you can take sex alone and somehow use sex and be successful. Indeed, you cannot.[4]

~ Adrian Rogers

I will say to the prisoners, 'Go free!' and to those who are in darkness, 'Come out to the light!' They will be like sheep that graze on the hills.

~ Isaiah 49:9 GNT

If the Son [Jesus Christ] therefore shall make you free, ye shall be free indeed.

~ John 8:36

I have gained perfect freedom by following your teachings.

~ Psalm 119:45 CEV

To

Jimmy Horne and Frankie Harbeson

Two deacons at my first student pastorate (1968–1970) who were and remain outstanding Christian servants, leaders, and friends. Both they and their wives Sylvia and Ella have remained faithful to Calvary Baptist Church and the Lord Jesus Christ for over fifty years.

Unto these, the words of Jesus to the church at Philadelphia certainly apply: "Thou hast kept my word, and hast not denied my name" (Revelation 3:8). May God increase their 'tribe' not only at Calvary but among the saints at large.

Thank you, Jimmy and Frankie, for trusting me as a nineteen-year-old teenager to pastor Calvary Baptist and the patience, encouragement, help, and love exhibited to me while I did. That time was foundational to my calling to and work as a vocational evangelist.

In my distress I called to the Lord; he answered me and set me free.

~ Psalm 118:5 GNT

Contents

Foreword		xi
Preface		xiii
1	A Rose by Any Other Name	1
2	Going by the Book	4
3	The Hidden Trap	11
4	Playing with Fire	13
5	Taken Prisoner	19
6	The Big Jailbreak	24
7	The Red Lizard and the Ghost	35
8	Staying Free	37
9	Key Takeaways (Review)	43
10	To Change Means to Choose to Change	46

Foreword

We live in the most remarkable time in the history of the world! It wasn't long ago that what we considered "commonplace" technology and convenience would've been dismissed as the delusional imaginings of science fiction. Through ever more miniature and incredible devices, we are continually "connected" to and bombarded by information and media—we have far more choices than we have time. Yet with all our technological wonders, we seem to be increasingly "disconnected" from the people and things that truly matter most—especially in our family relationships and with our adolescent population.

After more than twenty years of treating adolescents for problems with thought patterns and sexual behavior, I have come to the conclusion that one of the greatest tragedies of pornography and all of its partners in the media world is that they disconnect the viewer from a mindful awareness of all the beauty, potential and power within himself and those around him. He sacrifices precious moments that could be filled with true peace, joy and fulfillment for the "robotic" pursuit of momentary sensation.

In this startling book on the impact that pornography has on the adolescent population, Frank Shivers is able to communicate not only the need to avoid this trap but also the importance of confronting it from a spiritual perspective. Pornography impacts an adolescent physically, emotionally and spiritually. This resource book provides the answer for addressing concerns in all of these areas, and it is only by addressing all three areas that the adolescent can overcome this addictive pattern of behavior.

Tim P. Faulk, Ph.D., LMFT
Board Certified Expert in Traumatic Stress
Board Certified in Sexual Abuse
1450 Ross Clark Circle, Suite 3
Dothan, Alabama 36301
334.794.2113; 334.702.1220 (Fax)

Preface

"The eye is the lamp of the body. If your eyes are healthy, your whole body will be full of light. But if your eyes are unhealthy, your whole body will be full of darkness" (Matthew 6:22–23 NIV).

Since my writing of *The Pornography Trap* a decade ago, not only has the sordidness and raunchiness of pornography worsened and expanded (every day there are 68 million search engine requests for pornography[5]), but its use among young men has escalated. A recent study revealed that 50 percent of teenagers and about 75 percent of young adults view pornography at least monthly.[6] In the United States, 70 percent of college students watch porn.[7] Every second on the internet there are roughly 28,000 users watching porn.[8]

The Poison of Porn is written to combat pornography's aggressive appeal to the sensual appetite of the flesh by helping young men know how to navigate safely away from it. I am indebted to Dr. Timothy Faulk for encouraging its writing.

Pornography, simply and concisely defined, is all obscene (filthy, indecent) sexual material. Its inlet into the mind are the eyes. Jesus says that in keeping the eyes healthy (uncontaminated with pornography), the whole body (one's life) will be healthy (full of light). The overarching purpose for this book is to help *young men and younger men* do just that—maintain morally clean eyesight so they may steer clear of the poison of pornography.

Pornography is epidemic. The number of its users is incalculable (perhaps as many as 40 million in America). Shockingly, 76 percent of Christian youth ages 18–24 actively seek out porn.[9] Pastors (57 percent of them) say porn addiction is the most damaging issue in their churches.[10] Pornography sites have more traffic that Netflix, Amazon and Twitter combined and generate more income than that of ABC, NBC and CBS put together.[11] Porn's availability, accessibility, affordability and anonymity contribute to its widespread usage at epidemic proportion.

> Porn's availability, accessibility, affordability and anonymity contribute to its widespread usage at epidemic proportion.

Prior to the arrival of the internet, the average age for the exposure to pornography was between the ages of 11 and 13. Now, some researchers (people who study things like this) state that it is down to age 8. In fact, ninety percent of students aged 8 to 16 have viewed pornography on the internet.[12] The largest group of viewers of internet pornography are children ages 12 to 17.[13] Children and young people are often introduced to pornography unintentionally by stumbling across its path in some form. To know that children and teens on the internet are only *two clicks* (websites) away from seeing pornography accidentally or intentionally is really scary and alarming.

Firm boundaries (self-imposed) enveloped this writing.

1. It would expose pornography's cause, curse and cure without detailing its raunchiness through inclusion of "examples" depicting its vile and distasteful material.
Diligent effort was made to make the book nothing more than "PG" in content (hopefully lower but certainly not higher).

2. It would be "readable" by the young.
Big words were laid aside for simpler ones or else defined when used.

3. It would be "understandable" to the young.
Effort was made to keep the "cookie jar on the lowest shelf." However, even in that attempt there may be words used and things written that are not understood. That's okay. In time all will be clear, but for the present there will be enough understood to protect from the poison and ruin of pornography.

Preface

4. It would be Biblically sound in its counsel and guidance.

The principles stated in this volume, though written to young men to help them abstain from, avoid and defeat pornography, are universally true, making it profitable reading for both genders of all ages in all places of the world.

A prayer for young men before going further in this book.

Lord Jesus, help the young men reading this book understand that pornography is designed and empowered by Satan for their destruction, that it's not a "pleasure" to enjoy but a "poison" to abhor and avoid. Give them the will power and strength to navigate their life far away from its every form.

Lord, only You can break the power of porn's grip upon a life. I pray for the young men reading this book who are addicted to porn (shackled with its chains mentally) that You will help them realize that real freedom is found in You, that the antidote to the poison of pornography is the blood of Jesus Christ. Lift them from despair by instilling hope for deliverance. Help them understand that with You in the equation, nothing is impossible, including forgiveness of and freedom from pornography. In Jesus' name break the chains that have a stranglehold on their minds, setting them free. On their behalf I claim Your promise of Luke 4:18, that You have come to set people like them free from captivity and bondage.

May all that walk through the pages of this book not only *ingest* its content but *digest* it so that they might *manifest* it through walking in freedom from pornography.

In Jesus' powerful and wonderful name I pray. Amen.

1

A Rose by Any Other Name

There is a mistaken view of pornography's nature (its "basic or inherent features, character, or qualities"—*Oxford Dictionary*) in that "seventy percent of teens and young adults define [it] by its function, not its form."[14] It is not defined first as material that is sexually graphic, but that intended to create sexual arousal.[15] This definition or belief *excludes* nudity or sexual content in a movie, etc., that doesn't inflame sexual urges (lust) as pornographic.[16] To most young men it's the purpose behind the viewing of an image (its function for the viewer) which determines something to be porn or not.[17]

The word *pornography* comes from two Greek words. First is the word *porne,* which refers to a prostitute (male or female). The second word is *graphe,* "meaning a picture, a painting, or a writing."[18] Simply put, pornography (its form, not just its function) is anything that is heard, read, said or seen that is indecent, lewd and obscene (erotic, offensive to moral principles—*Google Dictionary*). Based upon this definition, something doesn't have to incite lust or thirst for sexual gratification to qualify as porn—just be vulgar, foul and vile. It's both the *form* (sexually graphic image) and *function* (incites sexual arousal) that define material as pornographic. Whoever says that pornography is harmless or that it has a good use in society is not telling the truth.

> It's both the *form* (sexually graphic image) and *function* (incites sexual arousal) that define material as pornographic.

Pornography comes in many forms and various disguises, casting the impression that it is *safe* and *innocent*. But always remember, a rose by any other name is still a rose, and poison by any other name is still deadly. Porn by any other name or "appearance" is still highly toxic.

The Forms (Faces) of Pornography include:

Erotic Photos, Movies, Videos and DVDs

Obscene Magazines

Porn Video Games

Porn Spam (emails with pornographic communication) is received on a daily basis by 47 percent of school-aged children.[19] Porn spam will trick a person into opening its content by pretending to be something else.

Erotic Music

Internet Porn Websites (sexually explicit websites). These sites "lock" you in, once entered, by disabling options such as back, exit or close navigation button in the attempt to lure or force you to stay.

Chatrooms are visited by sexual predators. Pornography perpetuates the sexual exploitation of the young. Eighty-nine percent of sexual solicitations to youth are made in chatrooms.[20] One in five youth ages 10 to 17 have received a sexual solicitation or was approached while on the internet.[21] Chatrooms are frequented by adults pretending to be teens for the purpose of the sexual exploitation of the young. Pornography contributes greatly to and is itself a form of sex trafficking.

> Chatrooms are frequented by adults pretending to be teens for the purpose of the sexual exploitation of the young.

Never divulge personal information (name, age, address or phone number) to and absolutely never arrange a meeting with people met in chatrooms. Wisdom (the counsel of God) advises avoidance altogether of such places. See Proverbs 1:5 and Proverbs 2:10–18.

Cell Phone Pornography. Sixty-one percent of pornography is viewed on a cell phone.[22] Eighty-seven percent of university students have viewed sex over webcams or phones.[23] Despite the attempt of parents to provide their children protection from pornography by monitoring computer usage and installation of porn blockers (*bravo* for such parents), they have little control over its access via the cell phone. Therefore, youth must exhibit personal restraint in the use of cell phones for pornographic searches or purposes.

Xbox live. Dialog with and agreement to meet an unknown person on the device is extremely dangerous (it could result in being sexually exploited). Xbox can be kept safe through *uKnowKids,* which helps parents monitor their digital activities on iPhones, iPads, iPods, Android phones, and social media.

Public display of marital sexual relationship. In private, the sexual relationship between a married couple is wonderful (Hebrews 13:4), but a public display of it is woefully obscene (pornographic).

Sexting. The act of sharing or getting pornography on a cell phone (sexting) is not only wrong but unlawful (You could go to jail for doing it). One in five teens has engaged in sexting.[24]

Coarse sexual joking. Foul-mouthed (dirty, nasty, vulgar) sexual joking (pornographic talk) arouses urges that are immoral and creates a desire to hear or see more of the same. It is through this form of porn that many boys say they got "hooked" or enslaved to the need for it.[25]

Sleepovers or *campouts.* Introduction to or the escalation of involvement with porn often occurs in overnighters with friends. True friends don't pull you down morally (encourage porn access). The psalmist says, "Happy are those who don't listen to the wicked, who don't go where sinners go, who don't do what evil people do" (Psalm 1:1 NCV).

Homework web searches. Seventy percent of children 7 to 18 years old accidentally view online pornography, often through a web search while doing homework.[26] Extreme caution must be utilized for any travel (even good and wholesome) upon the internet highway.

> Everywhere you go on the internet, "footprints" are left. A better expression than "surfing the web" is "walking on the beach."

Everywhere you go on the internet, "footprints" are left. A better expression than "surfing the web" is "walking on the beach."[27] Wherever you go may be discovered, even if the *cache* files are deleted.[28]

Have you ever seen a sign that reads "No Dumping Allowed"? People post such signs on their property trying to keep people from dumping unwanted trash. A "No Dumping Allowed" sign should be hung (posted) in your heart to keep out pornography and literature of every sordid sort that the Devil wants to get in.

2

Going by the Book

Satan's aim is to get people to do exactly the opposite of what God teaches in His Word. In the Garden of Eden, Satan told Adam and Eve a lie—that it was okay to eat of the forbidden fruit. They believed him, ate of the fruit, and suffered for it. See Genesis 2:15–17; 3:1–7, 15; and 1 Corinthians 15:21–22. All who believe the lie of Satan rather than the Word of God likewise bear severe consequences presently and eternally.

Believe what Christ said before believing man, demons or Satan. He alone is *True Truth,* its embodiment and source. See John 14:6; 8:32. Therefore, that which He says (Holy Scriptures) is accurate beyond error (John 17:17) and is to be trusted to give guidance in navigating lifestyle and choices.

John MacArthur said, "In other words, the truth of Christ and the truth of the Bible are of the very same character. They are in perfect agreement in every respect."[29]

The Word of God trumps (overrules) culture, conscience, and conviction.

The B-I-B-L-E,
Yes, that's the Book for me.
I stand alone on the Word of God—
The B-I-B-L-E.

The biblical bases for abstaining from pornography are numerous. Note from among them twelve.

Jesus wants a person to be pure. He says, "They are blessed [happy] whose thoughts are pure [or whose hearts are pure; the pure in heart], for they will see God" (Matthew 5:8 EXB). Purity means to be right with God. It is related to cleanness and blameless, guiltless, and innocent behavior.[30] It is to exemplify integrity to the core of one's being. "A thing is pure when there is nothing in it out of harmony with its nature. Gold is pure when it has been separated by fire from all foreign matter. The diamond is pure, the crystal is pure, when there is nothing in them which hinders the reflection of light. It is thus with the heart. It is pure when it loves only that which it ought to love."[31]—and when nothing in it hinders the reflection of God's holy Light.

The Greeks used purity to refer to something physically clean—such as a cloth with no dirt clinging to it. They understood something to be pure when it was free from additives, things that would hinder it from being used for its designed purpose. Water that poisoned instead of nourished was not free to be the water it was created to be, nor a cloth bandage that infected rather than aided in healing free to be used as it was intended.[32]

A substance that was contaminated could be free to do its intended work once the interference was removed. You are pure before God when free from that sinful "additive" that hinders you from being what God intended. Satan will be vigilant to infiltrate your life with a "sinful additive" like pornography, robbing you of purity and God's divine design (plan).

The saying "garbage in, garbage out" (impacts attitudes and actions) is no truer than when it comes to the viewing of pornography. Determine to keep the *garbage* out of your life. Stay clean. With Paul, I exhort, "With eyes wide open to the mercies of God, I beg you, my brothers, as an act of intelligent worship, to give him your bodies, as a living sacrifice, consecrated to him and acceptable by him. Don't let the world around you squeeze you into its own mould, but let God re-mould your minds from within, so that you may prove in practice that the plan of God for you is good, meets all his demands and moves towards the goal of true maturity" (Romans 12:1–2 PHILLIPS).

> When something enters your mind and heart, it will affect you. We are the sum total of the thoughts that come in and go out of us. That's the reason we're warned against the poison of pornography.
> Adrian Rogers

What is seen impacts conduct. The most searched for word on the internet is "sex."[33] "Your eye is the lamp of your body. When your eye is healthy, your whole body is full of light, but when it is bad, your body is full of darkness" (Luke 11:34 ESV). Pornography is not uninfluential, despite belief to the contrary. Dr. Victor Cline reasons, "However, for someone to suggest that pornography cannot have an effect on you is to deny the whole notion of education or to suggest that people are not affected by what they read and see. If you believe that a pornographic book or film cannot affect you, then you must also say advertising has no effect on its readers or viewers. Astute (shrewd, clever) businessmen would not spend billions of dollars a year on advertising if their visual and verbal messages and imagery did not motivate people to buy deodorant or diapers or automobiles. The key question is not whether, but what kind of an effect does pornography have?"[34] Adrian Rogers wrote, "When something enters your mind and heart, it will affect you. We are the sum total of the thoughts that come in and go out of us. That's the reason we're warned against the poison of pornography."[35]

Pray unto the Lord with David, saying, "Don't let me look at worthless things" (Psalm 119:37 ERV). The eyes are like a camera, just much better. The way pornography gets into the head is through the eyes. Unlike pictures taken with a camera however, these pictures are hard to delete or erase.

Satan is behind the spread of pornography and its damaging impact upon people and societies. Satan is not one to be "toyed" with, for he possesses supernatural power. Paul says, "For we are not fighting against flesh-and-blood enemies, but against evil rulers and authorities of the unseen world, against mighty powers in this dark world, and against evil spirits in the heavenly places" (Ephesians 6:12 NLT). See 2 Corinthians 10:4–5; John 10:10 and 1 Peter 5:8–9. Obviously, anything that Satan is for, Christians should be against. Scripture says that Satan is "the prince of the power of the air" (Ephesians 2:2); therefore, it makes sense the "airways" would be used much by him to saturate the world with licentious, obscene material in an effort to thwart biblical morality. And it's working, for 40 million Americans "regularly visit porn sites."[36]

> The Bible could not be clearer: "Among you there must *not be even a hint* of any kind of impurity." I urge you to be honest about this and to turn from it—decisively and forcefully. Don't dabble with it; don't go near places where you'll be tempted to obtain it; avoid anything on the internet that even hints of it.
> Billy Graham

Flee Pornography. God's instruction concerning pornography is clear: run from it (2 Timothy 2:22). Billy Graham wrote, "The Bible could not be clearer: 'Among you there must *not be even a hint* of…any kind of impurity' (Ephesians 5:3 NIV). I urge you to be honest about this and to turn from it—decisively and forcefully. Don't dabble with it; don't go near places where you'll be tempted to obtain it; avoid anything on the internet that even hints of it."[37]

Lust is instilled (aroused) by obscene pictures. Ezekiel said, "But she carried her prostitution still further. She saw men portrayed on a wall, figures of Chaldeans portrayed in red, with belts around their waists and flowing turbans on their heads; all of them looked like Babylonian chariot officers, natives of Chaldea. As soon as she saw them, she lusted after them and sent messengers to them in Chaldea. Then the Babylonians came to her, to the bed of love, and in their lust they defiled her. After she had been defiled by them, she turned away from them in disgust" (Ezekiel 23:14–17 NIV).

Don't allow pornography to live in your head. "Above all else, guard your heart [head], for everything you do flows from it" (Proverbs 4:23 NIV). See Proverbs 6:25. Don't give place (opportunity for the Devil to work) to the Devil in your head (thoughts) by thinking about erotic or deviant pictures (Ephesians 4:27). Jesus warned against the lustful look, saying, "You have heard that it was said, 'You must not commit adultery.' But I tell you that if a man looks at a woman and wants to sin sexually with her, he has already committed that sin with her in his mind" (Matthew 5:27–28 ERV). See Ephesians 5:3.

> Never for a moment look at any picture that taints your imagination with evil suggestion.
> R. A. Torrey

R. A. Torrey, great theologian and pastor of the nineteenth century, states, "Never for a moment look at any picture that taints your imagination with evil suggestion. Avoid as you would poison every painting, every engraving, every etching, every photograph that leaves a spot of impurity on your mind; but feast your soul upon pictures that make you holier, kinder, more sympathetic, more tender, more like your Lord."[38]

Self-control and restraint sexually are not harmful but healthy. Porn teaches that sexual restraint is damaging physically and mentally (to the psyche). John Drakeford counters that lie, saying, "The biblical portrayal of sex leaves no room for the view that if an individual does not give expression to the libido forces in his personality, some sort of psychic damage may follow."[39] Some, Jesus noted, "made themselves eunuchs for the kingdom of heaven's sake" (Matthew 19:12). The reference would not have been made had their discipline not been virtuous and healthy. Jesus' point was that celibacy (chastity; abstinence from sexual relations outside marriage) was not only a "normal," but a healthy lifestyle.

Refuse to be led astray. The goal of young porn viewers (certainly not all) is to pull others down to their decadent (corrupt) "level" through introducing and influencing them to pornography. To see another defile his purity somehow validates the soiling of his own. Solomon says to turn your back on them and walk away (Proverbs 1:10).

> [God] wants you to be free to live life happily and meaningfully, unhindered by pornography or any other sin.

God's love is changeless. God's love is not based upon a person's conduct (good or bad) but His character (love). See 1 John 4:8. God loves you just as you are but loves you too much to let you remain that way, for He wants you to be free to live life happily and meaningfully, unhindered by pornography or any other sin. Jesus said, "The thief's (the Devil's) purpose is to steal and kill and destroy. My purpose is to give them a rich and satisfying life" (John 10:10 NLT).

What controls a person is his master. "They promise them freedom, but they themselves are not free. They are slaves of things that will be destroyed. For people are slaves of anything that controls them" (2 Peter 2:19 NCV). See Romans 6:16 and Matthew 6:24. He that Jesus sets free from pornography (as with all sin) is really free (John 8:36).

Must I in sinful bondage be
Deprived of peace and liberty,
When in the promise I can see
The blood of Jesus cleanseth [me]?

~ Barney E. Warren (1900)

Forgiveness for viewing pornography is readily available. "If we tell Him [Jesus] our sins, He is faithful and we can depend on Him to forgive us of our sins. He will make our lives clean from all sin" (1 John 1:9 NLV). The only sin Jesus will not forgive is the sin that is not confessed.

Before the throne of God above
    I have a strong, a perfect plea:
A great High Priest, whose name is Love,
    Who ever lives and pleads for me.

When Satan tempts me to despair
    And tells me of the guilt within,
Upward I look and see him there
    Who made an end of all my sin.

Because a sinless Savior died,
    My sinful soul is counted free;
For God, the Just, is satisfied
        To look on Him and pardon me
        To look on Him and pardon me.

Hallelujah! Hallelujah! Praise the One,
Risen Son of God!

~ C. L. Bancroft (composed in the 1860s)

After sinning, focus upon your guilt, for it leads to repentance, but more upon the grace of God, which leads to forgiveness and restoration.

> After sinning, focus upon your guilt, for it leads to repentance, but more upon the grace of God, which leads to forgiveness and restoration.

Prevention is better than cure. Avoid entanglement with porn. C. H. Spurgeon, the great London pastor, said never "tempt the Devil to tempt you. We are not to enter the woods in search of the lion. Prevention is better than cure: it is better to be so well-armed that the Devil will not attack you than to endure the perils [dangers] of the fight, even though you come off a conqueror."[40] An ounce of prevention is worth a pound of cure. Constantly pray, "Lead us not into temptation; but deliver us from evil [or the evil one, Satan]" (Luke 11:4).

Pornography, like illicit sex, is unfulfilling. The epistle of Jude summarizes that it is like clouds without water (vv. 12–13). It is filthy and defiling (v. 8). It brings inescapable shame like raging waves of the sea (v. 13). Its source, as with other sins, is the Devil (v. 6). It will be severely judged by God (vv. 14–16). Jude gives encouragement regarding any shameful, sinful conduct (including pornography), stating that the Lord Jesus Christ is able to keep a person from drinking from its poisonous cup, falling into its trap (v. 24). See Psalm 141:9–10.

3

The Hidden Trap

Bill Hybels tells of a person who wrote to him saying, "I am an emotional invalid. My addiction to pornography paralyzes my spiritual life, perverts my view of the world, distorts my social life, and destroys any possibility of God using me, and I just can't stop.

Lust eats me up, yet it doesn't satisfy. Pornography promises me everything; it produces nothing."[41]

The Bible book of James describes how pornography works. It says, "But people are tempted when their own evil desire leads them away and traps them. This desire leads to sin, and then the sin grows and brings death [great harm]" (James 1:14–15 NCV). F. B. Meyer illustrates the teaching of James by the use of botany: "You know that flowers have their sex and the bees gathering honey in one flower carry the pollen to another and the result is flower and fruit. Precisely in the same way the heart of man is always open, and bees of all kinds seem to bring the pollen of unholy thoughts. When these are sown in the desires of our nature, there is at once the result of which James speaks. As soon as you allow the evil thought to mingle with your nature, it bringeth forth the act of sin; and sin, when it is finished, bringeth forth death."[42]

Pornography's entrapment begins with an *allurement* into its den of iniquity through use of appetizing bait (that which is erotic and corrupt). The bait, if taken, *inflames lust* for the erotic and brings captivity to (domination by) it. Lust *gives birth to* sinful indulgences whose pleasure brings painful consequences.

The shackles and chains to porn are forged stronger by *choice* (continuation in partaking of its erotic food). Jerry Vines said, "Temptation is when Satan looks through the keyhole. Sin is when we open the door." The more often the door is opened to porn, the greater the incarceration.

> The more often the door is opened to porn, the greater the incarceration.

A young man was madly in love with a farmer's daughter, but the two were not permitted to date. In his anger about the refusal, the young man, under the cover of darkness, sowed Johnson grass seed in the farmer's field. The farmer never discovered the culprit of the prank.

In time the young man married the farmer's daughter and inherited the farm. The wild and troublesome seeds sown in his youth many years earlier, he sought to root up his entire adulthood. Sow the seed of pornography in the field of the heart now and you may be rooting it up the rest of your life. It may take just one pornographic seed sown to create a nightmare and bondage that will prove nearly inescapable.

Dr. Mark Schwartz said, "Sex on the Net is like heroin; it grabs them and takes over their lives. And it's very difficult to treat because the people affected don't want to give it up."[43]

Avoid the poison of pornography by disciplined restraint, not looking at *any* pornography (its enticing, luring, attracting bait).

4

Playing with Fire

King Solomon wrote, "Can a man scoop fire into his lap without his clothes being burned?" (Proverbs 6:27 NIV). It might read, "Can a person look at pornographic pictures without their being burned into the permanent memory bank of the mind, resulting in sexual misconduct time and again?" Both the Bible and human experience answer Solomon with a loud, "No!"

Bill Hybels wrote, "If pornography distorts the sexual perspective of adults, think what it must do to children who are incapable of making wise decisions about simple things, let alone something as complex as human sexuality."[44]

Porn is harmful to young men in at least eleven ways.

It colors life. Porn colors your life. Playing with sin is like playing with coal. It is impossible not to be colored with its nature. You may say, "Frank, this one thing won't hurt me. Everybody is doing it. One visit to a pornographic website won't harm me. One act of sexual immorality won't injure me."

You are wrong. Porn, regardless of its type or the number of times viewed, does hurt you; and it colors all of life.

Youth is the planting stage of life; adulthood is the reaping stage. You will always harvest what you plant, perhaps for the rest of your life. The Bible says, "Do not deceive yourselves; no one makes a fool of God. You will reap exactly what you plant" (Galatians 6:7 GNT). "One sin," says C. H. Spurgeon, "can ruin a soul forever; it is not in the power of the human mind to grasp the infinity of evil that slumbereth in the bowels of one solitary sin."[45]

It wastes time. Effort looking for "just the right kind" of pornography on the computer or in magazines is a waste of time. The time should be used doing homework, playing outdoors or reading the Bible—doing wholesome and helpful things.

It keeps you from being who God intended you to be. Looking at porn hinders you from growing spiritually (knowing Jesus better and becoming more like Him). "No one can have two bosses. He will hate the one and love the other. Or he will listen to the one and work against the other. You cannot have both God and riches as your boss at the same time" (Matthew 6:24 NLV). In looking at pornography, closeness with God decays (lessens) and one's walk with Him becomes cold and distant. Man "loses all reality…Satan does not fill us with hatred of God, but with forgetfulness of God."[46]

It changes values. Porn destroys moral and biblical values, causing a person to believe that what it depicts is acceptable behavior. The more often that porn is viewed, the more it alters beliefs about right and wrong—"garbage in, garbage out."

It rewires the brain. Repeated porn viewing literally causes the brain to rewire itself.[47] This rewiring forms new nerve (neuronal) pathways that make intense and lasting changes in the brain.[48] Think of "neuronal pathways" like a trail in the forest which, when traveled, gets wider and more permanent.[49] Similarly, when a message like porn travels a neuronal pathway, the pathway gets stronger and stronger and longer lasting.[50]

Porn activates the reward center of the brain, "triggering the release of a cocktail of chemicals that give you a temporary buzz."[51] One of the chemicals is *DeltaFosB*.[52] Liken it to a garrison of men with shovel and pick in hand, or beavers constantly clearing and grooming the "path" in the brain. "Basically, the *DeltaFosB* is saying, 'This feels good. Let's be sure to remember it so we can do it again.'"[53] The likelihood of this happening to a teen is especially "high because their reward center in the brain responds two to four times more powerfully than that of the adult's, releases higher levels of *dopamine* and *DeltaFosB*."[54]

"*DeltaFosB* is referred to as 'the molecular switch for addiction,'"[55] because if it builds up enough in the brain, it switches on genes that create long-term cravings, driving the user back for more.[56] "And once it has been released, *DeltaFosB* sticks around in the brain for weeks or months, which is why porn consumers may feel strong cravings for porn long after they've stopped the habit."[57] "These memories," states Victor Cline, "very vivid and graphic in nature, keep intruding themselves back on the mind's memory screen, serving to stimulate and arouse the viewer."[58]

Rob Jackson said, "Perhaps the most obvious injury from pornography occurs in the mind. Once porn is downloaded into our mental hard drive through the portals of the senses, it works like a computer virus, corrupting our thoughts about sexuality. The contaminated files include our thoughts about being male or female, what we believe about our sexuality, how we plan to behave sexually, and whether we have the capacity to remain faithful in marriage."[59] John Drakeford states, "The greatest casualties [to pornography] may be those from suggestive souls who gullibly swallowed [its] message and then were left with a sex hang-up that may be with them for all their days."[60]

> The greatest casualties [to pornography] may be those from suggestive souls who gullibly swallowed [its] message.
> John Drakeford

It causes shame and remorse. Pornography leads to shame and deep guilt that robs one of inner peace and joy. Some users of porn experience "depression, social isolation, damaged relationships," and additional sad consequences.[61] Isaiah says, "But the wicked are like the troubled [churning; storm-tossed] sea, [which] cannot rest [be quiet, at peace], whose waters cast up mire and dirt" (Isaiah 57:20). The antidote to shame and guilt is to navigate life away from porn, focusing continuously upon the Lord. "Thou [God] wilt keep him in perfect peace, whose mind is stayed on thee: because he trusteth in thee" (Isaiah 26:3).

It portrays the fictional as the real. Pornography tells lies (deceptive and destructive myths) about sex which are harmful not only now

> It may take Christian clinical counseling to "untwist" the twisted misinformation about healthy sexual relationships that pornography has instilled.

but later in marriage. Its world is completely unreal (fictional). What it depicts are not normal sexual relations but "staged" and unnatural. Danny Huerta says, "When teens view pornography, they bond with an illusion, not a person."[62] It mispresents God's design (intent) for sex. And yet thirty-six percent of young adults look to porn as an instructor for sex.[63]

Pornography presents sex out of its divinely designed context (marriage). As Van den Haag stated, "Pornography severs sex from its human context. It reduces the world to orifices [an opening] and organs; incessant copulation [lovemaking; sexual relations] without apprehension, relationship or love. It's the bare sensation of pain and pleasure. This reduction of life to varieties of sex is but the spinning out of unreal fantasies [make-believe] which upset the burden of reality and individuality, of conflict and commitment, thought and consideration. People are literally devoured, tortured, mutilated and dehumanized."[64]

It may take Christian clinical counseling to "untwist" the twisted misinformation about healthy sexual relationships that pornography has instilled.

> Pornography has a detrimental effect on marriage, making those abusing it become incapable of having meaningful intimate relationships.
> Josh McDowell

Healthy relationships are difficult, if not impossible, for users of porn. Pornography spoils God's design of honor, happiness and holiness for the family. Its usage increases the marital infidelity rate by more than 300%.[65] In homes where it is allowed to exist relationships crumble. Covenant Eyes reports that 56 percent of divorce cases involve a partner's obsessive interest in porn sites.[66] Josh McDowell states, "Pornography has a detrimental effect on marriage, making those abusing it become incapable of having meaningful intimate relationships."[67]

Parents need to help their sons understand what a good, wholesome relationship looks like to counter that which porn advocates and produces.

It depreciates women. It degrades women into sex objects. Pornographers present women as "sex things," not the majestic pearl of awesome value God created. Viewers of porn develop an unhealthy and highly toxic view of women.

THE POISON OF PORN

It fuels illicit sex. Pornography fuels lust that seeks gratification through immoral and perverted sexual behavior. See I Thessalonians 4:3; Matthew 5:27–28 and Romans 1:24–27. Dr. James Dobson states that pornography leads to premarital sex, unprotected sex, prostitution, adulterous affairs, and problems during marriage. John Piper defined lust as "a sexual desire minus honor and holiness."[68] Frederick Buechner declared, "Lust is the ape that gibbers in our loins. Tame him as we will by day, he rages all the wilder in our dreams by night. Just when we think we're safe from him, he lifts up his ugly head and smirks, and there's no river in the world flows cold and strong enough to strike him down."[69] A Faulkner character was asked his opinion of original sin. He replied, "Well, it's like this. I ain't got to, but I can't help it."[70] Buechner and the Faulkner character are wrong. The flesh shouts loudly that one can't help lusting ("strike him down"), but God says otherwise. See Colossians 3:5 and Galatians 5:16.

> Lust is a sexual desire minus honor and holiness.
> John Piper

It makes you its prisoner. Imprisonment or slavery to the desire for a *rush* that porn provides often occurs through sexually charged advertisements, chick flicks (romantic movies) and coarse sexual joking.[71] "To an enslaved brain, porn and sexual fantasies become as basic a need as food and water."[72] The "inerasable" imprints porn forges upon the mind make deliverance from its clutches extremely difficult at best, for its chains are forged (made) with the strongest steel.

Escape is possible only through the power of Jesus Christ. "So if the Son [Jesus] makes you free, you will be truly free" (Romans 8:36 NCV).

> Pornography will take you farther than you want (intended) to go, cost you more than you want to pay and keep you longer than you want to stay.

A camel and his master spent the night in the desert. As the night unfolded, it became extremely cold, prompting the camel to seek permission to stay in the master's tent. At the first, only his head was allowed entrance. After more persistent begging and persuasion, the camel's shoulders gained entrance. Begging more, the master allowed the camel's entire body entrance. The camel then said, "There's not enough room in here for both of us, so you have to leave." Pornography works in that same fashion. If you gradually give place to it (little by little), eventually it will master you.

Pornography will take you further than you want (intended) to go, cost you more than you want to pay and keep you longer than you want to stay.

5

Taken Prisoner

"This has become the plague, the black hole, the bane of my existence, and I'm sick of it. I want ultimate freedom, victory and the ability to help others in their battle of sexual integrity, but at times I believe the enemy's lies that I'll never beat it. I want purity, righteousness and healing. It seems no matter how hard I try I can't completely break free, and I need help!"[73]

Pornography and sexual fantasies are addictive. Both are like lawn fertilizer that cause the soil to become dependent on it. In short-time time, the lawn won't grow without it.[74]

Sin (pornography) is at first a transgression (act of disobedience toward God), but it soon becomes a tyrant [cruel ruler, dictator]. William Clarkson states, "It [sin] grows into a power; and it becomes a power which holds the soul in its grasp, so that it is practically enslaved; it attempts to rise, to move, to do that which befits it and for which it was created, but it finds that it cannot; it is held down; its way is barred. This is true of sin in all its forms, and it is true in a number of degrees, varying from an objectionable constraint down to an almost hopeless despotism [oppressive absolute power and control by a sin]."[75]

Paul the Apostle echoes the same truth about man's inability in himself to thwart the power of any sin, including pornography. He writes, "I do not do the good I want to do. Instead, I am always doing the sinful things I do not want to do. If I am always doing the very thing I do not want to do, it means I am no longer the one who does it. It is sin that lives in me. This has become my way of life: When I want to do what is right, I always do what is wrong. My mind and heart agree with the Law of God. But there is a different law at work deep inside of me that fights with my mind. This law of sin holds me in its power because sin is still in me. There is no happiness in me! Who can set me free from my sinful old self? God's Law has power over my mind, but sin still has power over my sinful old self" (Romans 7:19–25 NLV). Sound familiar?

> Addiction means a person has no control over whether or not he or she looks at pornography.

You remember the "emotional invalid" who wrote to Bill Hybels about his "addiction to pornography" (chapter 3). For something to be "addictive" means that it takes control of a person to the point he just can't stop doing it. Alcohol and drugs are addictive by their intake into the body through the mouth, nose and needles. Pornography is addictive by its intake through the eyes. It is highly addictive because of chemicals (*dopamine* and *DeltaFosB*) that are released in the brain and cause a good feeling when viewing it.

You may not know that you are addicted (its prisoner, captive) to pornography until you try to stop viewing it without success.

In the classic movie *A Christmas Story*, during recess on a cold winter day, two boys surrounded by classmates argue whether a person's tongue will stick to the school's flagpole. One of the boys "triple-dog dares" the other to stick his tongue to the pole, and it gets stuck. As his classmates returned to class, there he remained with his tongue frozen to the flagpole in great pain. What in the world was the boy thinking? Obviously, he wasn't. He failed to ponder the consequence of the act.

That's the nature of pornography. Unthinkingly "sticking the tongue" to its "pole," you are bonded to it with incredibly strong adhesiveness.

Pornography's Modus Operandi (its ladder to entrapment)

There are four steps up the ladder to pornography addiction (control, domination, captivity).

The first step up the ladder is *Introduction*. The *gateway* into pornography is taking casual glances at it. These glimpses inflame (baits) the heart to desire a closer, longer, more private look.

The second step is *Escalation* (it increases). The law of "diminishing returns" occurs, for it takes more and more viewing of porn to create the same pleasure, due to the chemical CREB (Camp Response Element Binding protein). CREB attempts to put the brakes on the runaway train of porn in the brain by numbing a person's response to it.[76] Porn ceases to have the same effect, so users have to increase their porn intake to get aroused.[77]

According to tradition, this is how an Eskimo hunter kills a wolf. First, he coats the blade of a sharp knife with animal blood and allows it to freeze. Next, he adds layer upon layer of animal blood on the blade until the blade is completely concealed with frozen blood. The hunter then places the knife into the snow-covered ground with blade pointing upward. A wolf, picking up the scent of blood, locates the knife and licks it faster and faster, harder and harder, until its keen, razor-sharp edge is bare. His craving for blood masks the sting of the blade cutting into the mouth and the realization that the blood it now is licking is its own. Ultimately the wolf's carnivorous appetite for more and more blood ends in its death.

Man turns to pornography for the same reason the wolf licks the knife blade. It is appealing and appears to be pleasurable and harmless.

But soon the law of diminishing returns sets in, requiring more and more of the same to be satisfied. It's not one look at porn but three looks; not three looks but four.

Faster and harder one licks the deceptive bait blade of pornography until a crisis develops. The wolf didn't see coming what resulted, nor do those who take that first look and second look and…It's just the baiting scheme Satan uses to lure one into a snare, only then to destroy body, mind and soul. The law of sowing and reaping applies not only to seed planted in the soil but in the heart (Galatians 6:7). This law clearly teaches that a person may choose the seed he plants in the sod of the soul, but he cannot choose its outcome. A person always reaps what is sown whether desired or detested.

The third step is *Brainwashing*. Psychologists call it *Desensitization*. Those at this step see nothing wrong with what they view or do in regard to pornography, even though at the first they did. The filth of pornography gradually takes control of their mind. What they thought was disgusting and sickening at the first becomes acceptable. Numbness (no discomfort or guilty feeling) regarding pornography takes place. Eighty percent of porn users feel no guilt about using it,[78] having had their consciences "seared" or hardened to its wrongness. Paul says they "cannot see what is right and what is wrong. It is as if their understanding were destroyed by a hot iron"

(1 Timothy 4:2 ICB). It leaves them "incapable of ethical functioning" (1 Timothy 4:2 AMP).

> It makes no difference if one is an eminent physician, attorney, minister, athlete, corporate executive, college president, unskilled laborer, or an average fifteen-year-old boy. All can be conditioned into deviancy.
> Victor B. Cline, Ph.D.

Dr. Victor B. Cline said, "It makes no difference if one is an eminent physician, attorney, minister, athlete, corporate executive, college president, unskilled laborer, or an average fifteen-year-old boy. All can be conditioned into deviancy."[79]

The fourth and top step of the ladder is *Participation*. In time the porn addict or prisoner reaches a point where the viewing of pornography no longer satisfies. Unsatisfied sexual urges pressure addicts to search out ways to fulfill sexual fantasies (mental thoughts; imaginations) with others. Soon these addicts move from paper and internet screen images to acting out the images to be sexually fulfilled. It is at this step that various violent sex crimes occur. A prominent law official said, "Not everyone who reads pornography is a sexual deviant, but all sex deviants read it."[80]

> Not everyone who reads pornography is a sexual deviant, but all sex deviants read it.

Psychologist Dr. James Dobson summarizes, "Pornography addiction causes people to become desensitized to the material, no longer getting a thrill from what was once exciting. They also fantasize about acting out various pornographic scenes; show callousness toward ordinary sexual relationships; become reclusive, attempting to hide the habit from family or friends; view the opposite sex as an object; and view sex as being solely for the pleasure of himself or herself."[81]

Don't underestimate the power of pornography to imprison. Just as an ocean begins with a drop of water and a stone is first a little pebble, a life ruined and enslaved to pornography begins with a first glance.

Oh, be careful little eyes what you see;
Oh, be careful little eyes what you see,
For the Father up above
is looking down in love.

Everyone riding the roller coaster of porn, with its highs and lows, will bottom out at some point and want to jump off. But the pull of pornography keeps one on the roller coaster. Get off it before it derails, destroying your life. The next chapter details how.

6

The Big Jailbreak

"Let's not pretend this is easier than it really is. If you want to live a morally pure life, here's what you have to do: You have to blind your right eye the moment you catch it in a lustful leer. You have to choose to live one-eyed or else be dumped on a moral trash pile" (Matthew 5:29–30 MSG).

A teenager testified, "Pornography is like a parasite, draining the goodness and life out of me, slowly but surely turning me into some instrument of decadence that I myself cannot recognize. I only pray that God has mercy on my soul and gives me the strength to break free."

Due to the low water level at a lake, a backhoe (a machine that digs up things) dug out the sand at the water-slide landing. The backhoe got "stuck" in a rut (hole) of its own making, and the more it sought to be freed, the more entrenched (deeper) it became in the sand. You might be like that backhoe, having gotten "stuck" in a rut of your own making regarding pornography. And trying harder to break free only leads to going deeper in it. The backhoe, with human help, was freed to accomplish its mission! With help, you can be set free from the quicksand (trap) of pornography to accomplish yours.

Pornography need not have the final say in your life. It can be thwarted never again to oppress or possess. How do you beat porn obsession or addiction?

Own up to the problem. To admit having a problem with pornography is not easy but is necessary to be set free from its power.

Change strategy (plans). To do what you have always done to stop looking at pornography (without success) will get what you have always gotten—defeat. Implement renewed effort with new tactics (see the following).

Repent. Feeling guilty or remorseful over the viewing of pornography is not synonymous (same thing as) with repentance. (That is, simply telling God that you're sorry for looking at porn is not repentance.) Repentance involves turning (180-degree turnabout) from something (sin) to Someone (Jesus). To repent is to express woeful sorrow for an action (heartfelt confession) unto the Lord, coupled with a serious intent to change conduct. It is to say with the prodigal son, "I have sinned," with the honest intent no longer to live in the pigpen of wickedness (pornography, etc.). See Luke 15:18;21.

Stop reinforcing porn pathways in the brain. The good news is that the pathways porn forms in the brain will dissipate and disappear if they aren't reinforced and are replaced with something else.[82] (Replace porn's place in your life with Bible study, hiking, sports, exercise, homework, etc.) Evil habits (like any others) are broken one day at a time. Don't be anxious or despair about tomorrow's battle. Just fight off the urge through Christ today. Victory *today* provides strength for tomorrow's battle. See Matthew 6:34.

Practice fasting. Isaiah says, "Is not this the fast that I have chosen? to loose the bands of wickedness, to undo the heavy burdens, and to let the oppressed go free, and *that ye break every yoke*?" (Isaiah 58:6). A yoke is a habitual indulgence (addiction) that seemingly cannot be broken. Biblical fasting can break its hold. Mind you, it's not the formality (going through the motions without earnestness of soul) of the fast (just abstaining from porn) that breaks its yoke of bondage, but the power of the Holy Spirit released upon doing it through heartfelt request.

Certainly, coupled with spiritual fasting is the fast of deprivation of the indulgence. With regard to porn, it (fast of deprivation) means abstaining from use of the internet (computer or phone) and other venues where porn may be accessed, until porn's grip is broken. Such "fasts" would be drastic and difficult but may be necessary if pornography is deeply rooted.

He breaks the power of canceled sin;
    He sets the prisoner free.
His blood can make the foulest clean;
    His blood availed for me. ~ Charles Wesley (1739)

Make yourself accountable. Since looking at porn is wrong, it often is a *secret* untold and unknown. In fact, it is so hidden that parents, closest friends and the youth minister may be "clueless" that it is viewed. Help awaits in courageously voicing your porn problem to one or more of them. Don't feel embarrassed or fearful. Additionally, Christian licensed clinical therapists (counselors that help people with their pornography habit) can provide invaluable help. See James 5:16 and Galatians 6:2.

God gave Gideon three hundred men to help him drive the enemy out of the land (Judges 7:7). Likewise, God will provide helpers (accountability partners) to assist in driving porn out of your life (v. 4).

What does an accountability relationship involve? What does it look like? How does it "play out"? Alan Medinger provides an answer:

"An accountability relationship is one in which a Christian gives permission to another believer to look into his life for purposes of questioning, challenging, admonishing, advising, encouraging, and otherwise providing input in a way that will help the individual live according to Christian principles that they both hold."[83] See Ephesians 5:19.

> An accountability relationship is one in which a Christian gives permission to another believer to look into his life for purposes of questioning, challenging, admonishing, advising, encouraging, and otherwise providing input in a way that will help the individual live according to Christian principles that they both hold.
> Alan Medinger

Fighting it alone results in defeat. Hebrews says, "And let us consider and give attentive, continuous care to watching over one another, studying how we may stir up (stimulate and incite) to love and helpful deeds and noble activities" (Hebrews 10:24 AMPC). Who might be the person(s) to render help in overcoming pornography's grip for you?

Replace the inferior with the superior. In his book *Future Grace*, John Piper writes: "We must fight fire with fire. The fire of lust's pleasures must be fought with the fire of God's pleasures. If we try to fight the fire of lust with prohibitions and threats alone—even the terrible warnings of Jesus—we will fail. We must fight it with the massive promise of superior happiness. We must swallow up the little flicker of lust's pleasure in the conflagration [massive destructive firestorm] of holy satisfaction. Our aim is not merely to avoid something erotic but to gain something excellent."[84]

To summarize, God alone provides genuine, forever, utmost happiness. Taste it, see it and you will believe it (Psalm 34:8). Turn your back on the temporal and destructive pleasure of pornography to embrace that which is far superior in every way. Replacing the inferior (lustful pleasure) with the superior (God's pleasure) results in true freedom. See John 10:10.

Don't think the problem will just go away. Pornography deceives you into thinking that in time the desire to look at it will disappear, that you will wake up one day never wanting to look at it again. Wrong. The truth is that without help now the problem only gets bigger and bigger.[85] Most adults "addicted" (controlled by; cannot stop looking) to pornography were introduced to it as a child or young man.

Rely upon Jesus. Jesus loves you and wants to help you stop looking at porn. Invite Him to come into your heart, forgive all the wrong you have done (sin), taking control of your life as Lord and Savior. The Bible says, "For everyone who calls on the name of the Lord will be saved from the punishment of sin" (Romans 10:13 NLV). Jesus will not only forgive all the bad stuff (sin), but will help you not do it again. "This means that anyone who belongs to Christ has become a new person. The old life is gone; a new life has begun!" (2 Corinthians 5:17 NLT). Rely upon Christ for power to withdraw from and resist pornography. You have natural strength, Satan has supernatural strength, but Jesus has *super-duper-natural strength.* Claim and walk in the promise of Philippians 4:13, which says, "I can do all things through Christ who strengthens me" (NKJV). Others may fail you. Jesus never will. Look to Him, and in being set free, you will sing with Chris Tomlin, "My chains are gone; I've been set free."

A little girl was once asked, "If Satan were to come to your house and knock at your door, what would you do?"

She answered, "I would not open the door myself. When Satan knocks at my door, I will send the Lord Jesus to the door, and when the Devil sees Him, he will run away! Jesus is my Savior and the One who protects me." Treat Satan in the same manner.

Obviously Christians may also be addicted to pornography. Sadly, many are at present. They testify with Paul, "When I want to do good, I don't; and when I try not to do wrong, I do it anyway. Now if I am doing what I don't want to, it is plain where the trouble is: sin still has me in its evil grasp" (Romans 7:19–20 TLB). The grappling hook of pornography refuses to let them go, despite their desperate attempts for freedom.

The Holy Spirit empowers the believer, enabling victory over the deeds of the flesh. You are infilled with the Holy Spirit upon dethroning self and sin from the throne in the heart, allowing Jesus Christ to rule supreme. See Luke 11:11–13. It is allowing the Holy Spirit not merely to be resident in the heart, but its President. As one walks in the Spirit (under His control), he will not fulfill the lust or urge of the flesh to do wrong (Galatians 5:16). It is therefore imperative that you daily say, "I will set my mind on the things of the Spirit" (Romans 8:5).

> The battle is nearly always won in the mind. It is by the renewal of our mind that our character and behavior become transformed.
> John Stott

John Stott, English theologian, advises "It is not enough to *know* what we should be.... We must go further and set our minds upon it. The battle is nearly always won in the mind. It is by the renewal of our mind that our character and behavior become transformed. So, Scripture calls us again and again to mental discipline in this respect. Self-control is primarily mind-control. What we sow in our minds, we reap in our actions."[86] It is for this reason that Paul admonishes believers that "have been raised with Christ [saved from the penalty and power of sin], [to] seek the things that are above, where Christ is, seated at the right hand of God. Set your mind on things that are above, not on things that are on earth. For you have died, and your life is hidden with Christ in God" (Colossians 3:1–3 ESV). See Romans 8:5–6 and Philippians 4:8.

Teach us to pray that we may cause
    The enemy to flee,
That we his evil pow'r may bind,
    His prisoners to free.
Teach us to pray and firmly stand
    Upon the battleground,
To fight and break the stronghold down,
    The enemy confound.
Teach us to pray and use Thy rod
    In strong, prevailing prayer,
Beneath Thy blood to shake the earth
    And powers of the air.
By prayer and faith, oh, may we learn
    To labor, Lord, with Thee,
To know the victory is ours
    And Thine authority.[87] ~ Watchman Nee

Daily quiet time with the Lord. Every day read the Bible and talk to Jesus, for both give strength to say no to the Devil when tempted to look at porn. A person attempting to explain to a missionary the inner struggles of the flesh warring against the Spirit said it was like a white dog and black dog fighting constantly. When asked which dog wins, the man replied, "The one I feed the most."

In the warfare of right against wrong (looking at pornography or not), the one you feed the most will win. Starve the black dog and feast the white dog and you will be victorious. Habits, good or bad, are formed by choice.

While flying, a pilot began to hear a rat gnawing away at something in the plane. Afraid that those gnawing teeth could cause the plane to crash, he remembered that rats can live only in the lowlands, not in the heights. He took the plane up higher and higher until the rat died. Pornography's gnawing at your heart cannot survive when you are soaring high with Jesus. It cannot stand the holy heights and eventually will die. Soar high with Jesus, and the problem with pornography will stop.

Memorize Scripture. "His [God's] cure is to keep your thought life immersed in His Word."[88] David said, "Thy word have I hid in mine heart, that I might not sin against thee" (Psalm 119:11). Did you know that Jesus quoted Scripture to the Devil in the wilderness when the Devil tried to get Him to do something wrong? And the Devil was defeated. Learn (memorize) Bible verses to say to the Devil when he tries to get you to look at pornography. Here are a few to hide in your heart: Romans 8:6; 2 Corinthians 10:4–5; Ephesians 4:27; 1 Peter 2:11; Job 31:1; Habakkuk 1:13 and Romans 6:16. Write them down on cards and keep saying them out loud until they are burned into the memory for easy recall when you are tempted.

Avoid urge triggers. There are things that bring on the urge to look at pornography or do bad things. We call these things "triggers." The Israelites had a problem with idolatry (worship of false gods made by man). To stop that worship, they had to "cut down" the groves of Baal (the places where they worshipped false gods), for as long as the groves remained, the Israelites would have opportunities to stumble back into idolatry (Judges 6:25). What they had to do to be set free from idol worship you must do to be set free from looking at pornography. Remove anything from your bedroom or school locker that the Devil can use to cause you to look at pornography again. Delete stored pornography web sites from the computer and destroy porn magazines and videos. Consider moving the computer to a family room where internet viewing is not private.

"Do not give the Devil an opportunity" (Ephesians 4:27 NET) to cause you to stumble back into pornography's trap. Remove yourself from that which fuels (triggers) the urge. Ask your parents to install *Forcefield*, the preferred parental control software solution of Focus on the Family. Check it out at http://fotf.forcefield.me for free for thirty days (offer at the time of this writing). *Net Nanny* (NetNanny.com) is another child porn blocker program.

Farmers place "blinders" on mules to force their focus on the furrow (row) being plowed. This device prohibits the mule from looking to the left or right, keeping him on course. Constantly put on "blinders," asking God to keep you from looking at pornography. Starve yourself from bad "eye candy."

Practice urge surfing. Psychologists (trained people that help people like you get freedom from pornography) call coping with pornography temptation "urge surfing."[89] It is like riding out a huge wave on a surfboard in the ocean. When the urge to look at pornography rises on the wave, ride the wave all the way through until the urge is gone. Stay on the surfboard (urge control) without falling into the water (pornography), and you beat the urge. Riding waves of temptation at times may seem to last a lifetime, but most come and go quickly (five seconds to five minutes). Each "wave" you champion builds spiritual muscle and resiliency to enable the riding of the next.

Change the focus. Upon being tempted to look at pornography or do bad things, shift thoughts or attention to Jesus, asking for strength to resist (not give in to) the urge. Fix [turn] your eyes on Jesus (Hebrews 12:2).

Tony Evans elaborates: "The way you get rid of sin is not simply dealing with or focusing on the sin. It's like being on a diet and deciding to focus on food all the time—it won't work. Instead, to deal with temptation, we must shift our focus. Rather than keeping our eyes on our sin, we need to turn our eyes to our Savior. As we focus on him and not on our Romans 7 experience, we find the freedom to overcome. Don't look at your sin. Look to your Savior."[90] 'And he that the son [Jesus] sets free shall be free indeed' (John 8:36). Adrian Rogers advises, "How are you going to think pure thoughts? By trying not to think impure thoughts? No. By thinking God's thoughts—not just pure thoughts."[91] See Philippians 4:8.

Turn your eyes upon Jesus;
Look full in His wonderful face....
His Word shall not fail you, He promised;
Believe Him, and all will be well. ~ Helen Howarth Lemmel (1922)

Sow good seed instead of the bad. The apostle Paul states, 'Do not sow unto the flesh' (Galatians 6: 8). That is, don't plant the seeds of pornography in your head by looking at pornography. Instead, plant good and helpful seeds in your head that will keep the bad seeds out. The reason you keep looking at pornography is that you keep planting the wrong seeds in the field of your heart. So say no to the bad seeds (you only position yourself for defeat when you don't) and yes to the good seeds to win over pornography. Substitute the bad (sinful) seeds with good (godly) seeds.

Zero tolerance toward pornography. Daily have a "zero tolerance" towards pornography. Deny the "one more time" syndrome (I'll look just one more time). Bring *every thought into captivity* [under His control] to Christ Jesus (2 Corinthians 10:4–5).

The five-second rule. The first five seconds of temptation often decide if you will give in to it or not. At the moment of pornography temptation, breathe a word of prayer for help and make a quick exodus from the scene.

Never concede defeat. Continually failing in your effort to permanently be set free from the clutches of pornography may lead to utter hopelessness that it will ever happen (a lie of Satan implanted in the mind). No matter how many times you fail in the battle for freedom, don't concede defeat. Victory is attainable. It is reachable. It is a winnable war. Multitudes even more entrenched in the quicksand of porn than you are have been rescued and set free. Banish the enemy's lie that though others have been set free, you cannot. No man is beyond the reach of the outstretched hand of Jesus Christ that pulls man from the miry clay of addiction and sets his feet upon "the solid Rock" (Psalm 40:2) to stay.

> No matter how many times you fail in the battle for freedom, don't concede defeat. Victory is attainable. It is reachable. It is a winnable war.

Upon man's cry for rescue, Christ bows His ear immediately to the petitioner's mouth ("He inclined unto me"—Psalm 40:1), granting deliverance through His bountiful mercy and forgiveness. "Prayer brings God down to help. His hand reaches to the man imprisoned in a pit or struggling in a swamp; the victim is dragged out, is set on a rock, and feels firm ground beneath his feet."[92] See Psalm 40:2.

From sinking sand, He lifted me;
With tender hand, He lifted me.
From shades of night to plains of light,
Oh, praise His name, He lifted me. ~ Charles H. Gabriel (1856–1932)

Exhibit determination. The white ermine (also called stoat) is hunted for its beautiful white fur. The hunter locates the ermine's home and pours tar (the black stuff used on roads) in front of it. When the dogs chase the ermine back to its home, it refuses to go through the tar to safety. Exposed, it is then killed by the hunter. The ermine would rather die than defile its beautiful white fur. Determine never again to be made unclean in your heart with the filthy, black tar of pornography. At all cost protect your "beautiful white" heart from it.

When knocked down, get back up immediately. Don't quit or despair. Regardless of numerous failures to thwart the temptation, never lose hope. Jesus' victory over the Devil at the cross assures your own victory through Him. With Paul, believe and say determinedly "I can do all things [including thwarting temptation] through Christ which strengtheneth me" (Philippians 4:13). Freedom from defeat is awaiting in the authority and power of Jesus Christ. Cease allowing Satan to intimidate and dominate. It's time to say, "Enough is enough."

To stay free, you have to protect your eyes from seeing pornography. It boils down to self-control rather than self-gratification. See Proverbs 4:23. What are some things that might be done to do that?

7

The Red Lizard and the Ghost

In C. S. Lewis' allegory (a story within a story that uses symbolic fictional characters to reveal a spiritual or moral truth[93]) *The Great Divorce,* lust is pictured as a red lizard sitting on a ghost of a man's shoulder, constantly whispering seductively into his ear. In time an angel, seeing the man with the lizard (lust) was distraught, asks, "Shall I kill it?" The man responds with uncertainty, struggling with his love for it and at the same time hatred for it. Excuse after excuse for delaying the death of the lizard is put forth to the angel by the man ("He's asleep now, not bothering me"; "I will break free from its grip gradually," "Tomorrow I will let you kill it," etc.). He wants it killed, but not "today." In response, the angel forcefully said, "There is no other day. All days are present now. I cannot kill it against your will. It is impossible. Have I your permission?"[94]

Finally, the man grants permission to the angel to slay the lizard (lust). "Do what you like," he said, but ended, whimpering, "God help me. God help me."[95] The next moment the ghost (*man*) gave a scream of agony such as I never heard on Earth. The Burning One (angel) closed his crimson grip on the reptile, twisted it while it bit and writhed, and then flung it, broken-backed, on the turf."[96] Once the grip of lust was overcome, the ghostly man is transformed wondrously into a real man. The red lizard (lust) is transformed into a white stallion upon which the man mounts and rides upward to the mountain of God.

Later in the book, Lewis makes crystal clear the meaning of the allegory. Man may escape the gripping domination of lust only through spiritual death (not resolution, therapy or self-help books, though such may be helpful). Death to lust and its pleasures makes *real* life possible. Paul bears witness to this truth: "Don't be controlled by your body. Kill every desire for the wrong kind of sex. Don't be immoral or indecent or have evil thoughts" (Colossians 3:5 CEV). The Amplified Bible renders the text, "So *put to death and deprive of power the evil longings* of your earthly body [with its sensual, self-centered instincts] immorality, impurity, sinful passion, evil desire, and greed, which is [a kind of] idolatry [because it replaces your devotion to God]." To conquer lust, it will require sitting in an "electric chair" daily, dying to it and that which spurs it (pornography, etc.). Paul said, "I die daily" (1 Corinthians 15:31). If a spiritual giant like him had to die daily to sin, how much more must you and I.

When one declares death to lust and pornography in the name of Jesus, its prison cell is immediately opened, freeing man to live as God intended—happily, holily and wholesomely. Every effort for a jailbreak without the Lord sitting upon the throne in the heart is futile.

Lewis states, "What is a lizard compared to a stallion? Lust is a poor, weak, whimpering, whispering thing compared with that richness and energy of desire which will arise when lust has been killed."[97]

"Will you come with me to the mountains? It will hurt at first, until your feet are hardened. Reality is harsh to the feet of shadows. But will you come?"[98] With Lewis I ask, will you come to the mountain of bountiful joy and blessing by granting permission to the Lord to destroy the "lizard" of lust that constantly sits upon your shoulder?

The time for such a decision is today, not tomorrow or the day after. The lizard (lust) must be killed (totally obliterated) here and now!

8

Staying Free

"Christ has freed us so that we may enjoy the benefits of freedom. Therefore, be firm in this freedom, and don't become slaves again" (Galatians 5:1 NOG).

"So let the man who feels sure of his standing today be careful that he does not fall tomorrow" (I Corinthians 10:12 PHILLIPS).

> Pornography is an endless battle, but a winnable one.

"A Christian life," states Watchman Nee, "is an unending engagement on the battlefield."[99] The times that is forgotten will result in defeat by the enemy (Satan). A veteran missionary in his eighties was asked, "Tell me, when did you get beyond the problem with lust?" He responded, "It hasn't happened yet. The battle still goes on."[100] Don't be deceived by times when it is absent. Don't ever count it knocked out and dead. It has stubborn resiliency and will not quit in its effort to trip us up. Therefore, stay alert, for in such an hour when you think not, lust will show its ugly head through a sexual advertisement, image, movie or magazine endeavoring to pull you back into pornography. Pornography is an endless battle, but a winnable one.

Armor is a special kind of suit worn for protection. Football players wear a type of armor for protection on the gridiron, and catchers wear such in the game of baseball. As a baseball catcher, my armor consisted of a chest protector, shin guards, mask, and, of course, a glove. This armor kept me from serious injury and kept me in the game. Ephesians 6 states that, in the same way that athletes need armor for protection in athletic contests, Christians need spiritual armor for protection in the game of life—battling against the Devil and things like pornography.

A long time ago, for protection, Roman soldiers going into battle wore clothing called armor. They wore a helmet to protect their head (from rocks thrown, arrows shot, swords swung), a belt to keep all the parts of their bodily uniform (armor) in place (a sheath or long thin cover for the blade of a sword hung upon the belt, as did "strips of leather to protect the lower body."[101] The belt "girds on [secures] all the other pieces of our armor."[102]), shoes that would keep them from falling, a breastplate to protect (shield) the heart (front side of their body), a large shield to protect their face and head, and they carried a sword with which to fight. Note, that there was no provision for the back.

"Put on the whole armor of God, that ye may be able to stand against the wiles of the devil" (Ephesians 6:11). "The first step to being strong is to realize that life is not an encounter group. Life is not a bonding meeting. Life is not a playground. Life is a battleground. The reason so many in the church are weak is because they're not armed for battle."[103] We must "take advantage of the equipment God has given us to navigate life and negotiate the war that surrounds us."[104]

Knowing we would have to battle the Devil all the time, God gave us special armor so we could be victorious (win over the Devil). Unlike the Roman soldiers' armor (or an athlete's protective gear), it's invisible (cannot be seen). It is spiritual, not physical. You put it on by praying, trusting God and reading the Bible.

The Belt of Truth pictures the need to know what truth is, as taught in Holy Scripture, and to walk in it. It is important to read the Bible daily and seek to live out its teaching. The Bible shows what is right, what is not right, how to become right, and how to stay right. And it will help keep you right. David tells us that the Bible will keep a person from doing wrong (like looking at pornography). He says, "I have thought much about your words and stored them in my heart so that they would hold me back from sin" (Psalm 119:11 TLB). Like the sheath on the soldiers' belts that held the sword, truth allows us to carry the Sword and use it effectively.[105] Neil Anderson remarks, "Because Satan's primary weapon is the lie, your defense against him is the truth."[106]

> Because Satan's primary weapon is the lie, your defense against him is the truth.
> Neil Anderson

The Breastplate of Righteousness pictures dependence on Jesus, not yourself, to be clean, pure and holy. Every time pornography is viewed, immediately tell Jesus you're sorry, asking for cleansing and strength to refrain when the temptation recurs. Jude says, "God is strong and can help you not to fall. He can bring you before his glory without any wrong in you and give you great joy" (Jude 24 ICB).

The Gospel Shoes picture your "surefootedness" (peace, trust, calm assurance) in Jesus in battling the Devil, and your desire to tell others the story of Jesus with courage. Reliance (trust) placed in Jesus will help you "stand firm" (without slipping or stumbling into pornography or other wrongs).

The Shield of Faith pictures the need to always trust God no matter what the Devil or bad friends say. Genesis 3 records how Satan lied to Eve. "'You won't die!' the serpent replied to the woman. God knows that your eyes will be opened as soon as you eat it, and you will be like God, knowing both good and evil. The woman was convinced. She saw that the tree was beautiful and its fruit looked delicious, and she wanted the wisdom it would give her. So she took some of the fruit and ate it" (verses 4–6, NLT). Eve believed Satan over God, the shield came down, and sin entered the world. Don't be like Eve; always believe and trust God, and He will keep you from stumbling back into pornography. He is more than able to keep Satan from harming you and causing you to stumble. See 1 John 4:4.

> The power of Satan is in the lie. If you remove the lie, you remove the power.
> Neil Anderson

Neil Anderson noted, "If I were to tempt you, you would know it. If I were to accuse you, you would know it. But if I were to deceive you, you wouldn't know it. The power of Satan is in the lie. If you remove the lie, you remove the power."

His banner over us is love;
    Our sword the Word of God.
We tread the road the saints before
    With shouts of triumph trod.
By faith they like a whirlwind's breath
    Swept on o'er every field;
The faith by which they conquered death
    Is still our shining shield.
On every hand the foe we find
    Drawn up in dread array;
Let tents of ease be left behind,
    And onward to the fray.
Salvation's helmet on each head,
    With truth all girt about,
The earth shall tremble 'neath our tread
    And echo with our shout.
To him that overcomes the foe
    White raiment shall be giv'n;

Before the angels he shall know
> His name confessed in heav'n.
Then onward from the hills of light,
> Our hearts with love aflame,
We'll vanquish all the hosts of night
> In Jesus' conquering name.

~ John Henry Yates (1837–1900)

The Helmet of Salvation pictures the Holy Spirit's presence and power in your life to protect from domination (control) by wrong "urges" and things like pornography. It allows into your head (brain) only clean thoughts, sights and sounds. Sit tight on your thoughts. Don't insert yourself into pornographic pictures through daydreaming or fantasizing about them.

> This [Holy Scripture], being hid in the heart, will preserve from sin (Psalm 119:11), and will mortify and kill those lusts and corruptions that are latent [dormant or hidden] there.
> Matthew Henry

The Sword of the Spirit pictures the power of Holy Scripture that defeats Satan's efforts to overthrow God's rule, will and work in your life. In the wilderness temptations, Jesus used the Sword of the Spirit (Scripture) to drive Satan back by declaring, "It is written…" (Matthew 4:1–11). "It is written" is like a dagger to Satan's heart. In temptation to look at pornography, quote Scripture to Satan which forces him to flee. The Bible says, "Resist [say a loud no, backing it up with Scripture] the Devil, and he will run away from you" (James 4:7 ISV). Matthew Henry remarks, "This [Holy Scripture], being hid in the heart, will preserve from sin (Psalm 119:11) and will mortify and kill those lusts and corruptions that are latent [dormant or hidden] there."[107] In temptation to return to pornography, quote Scripture to the Devil. It is a weapon that drives him back.

The Knees of Prayer also are a source of power, protection and provision for victory over the Devil. Prayer will be the key to remaining free from pornography (and other sin). Soldiers in battle stay in constant contact with their commander for instructions. As a soldier in the Lord's army, you must stay in continual communication with your commander, the Lord Jesus Christ, to achieve victory. Matthew Henry writes, "We must join prayer with all these graces for our defense against these spiritual enemies, imploring help and assistance of God as the case requires; and we must pray always. We must pray with all prayer and supplication, with all kinds of prayer: public, private and secret, social and solitary, solemn and sudden; with all the parts of prayer: confession of sin, petition for mercy, and thanksgivings for favors received."[108]

John Owen wrote, "If we do not abide in prayer, we will abide in temptation. Let this be one aspect of our daily intercession: 'God, preserve my soul, and keep my heart and all its ways so that I will not be entangled.' When this is true in our lives, a passing temptation will not overcome us. We will remain free while others lie in bondage."[109]

> You can stand against the wiles of the Devil—the cunning, clever attacks of Satan—only to the degree that you're protected with the whole armor of God.
> Jon Courson

No baseball catcher would think of getting behind the plate without protective equipment. No Roman solider would have dared enter battle without protective armor. No Christian should do battle with the Devil without it either (the Ephesians 6 kind). With it you will be a winner over the Devil; without it you will a loser. This armor, if worn (used), will keep you from falling back into the trap of pornography. Make use of all its defensive weapons to repel temptation and stratagems of the Devil.[110] No part of the Christian is to lie exposed to the enemy's attack. Jon Courson remarks, "You can stand against the wiles of the Devil—the cunning, clever attacks of Satan—only to the degree that you're protected with the whole armor of God."[111]

Amidst a thousand snares I stand
Upheld and guarded by Thy hand;
That hand unseen shall hold me still
And lead me to Thy holy hill.[112]

Neil Anderson said, "We have all the resources we need to win *every* battle. The only question is whether or not we will fight the battle the Lord's way, using the weapons, armor and strategy that come from Him."[113]

9

Key Takeaways (Review)

Key or central *takeaways* for continued meditation and application from this book include the following.

Pornography refers to material with erotic and obscene content. It includes "form" as well as "function."

Christians are to live privately and publicly so that there is not "even a hint" of impurity.

With regard to porn, *prevention* is always better than its *cure* (remedy).

The eyes are like cameras (only superior) that take sharp and lasting pictures and videos, storing them within itself (chamber) for reviewing at any time. Unlike a camera, however, pictures and videos taken with the "camera of the eye" are not easily deleted or erased.

You cannot *unsee* what is seen. And that which is viewed may require the help of a licensed Christian therapist to overcome or get past. Though preferably not needed, this is okay. A doctor is summoned when the body is sick or hurt. A Christian therapist or counselor is summoned when the *mind* is hurt. Both know how to help us recover.

Pornography is addictive (something it is difficult to stop). It controls its consumer. It is understandable why porn has been called the "new drug," for almost immediately it *chains* its user to itself like heroin or other chemical drugs shackles their users. Failure in the effort to stop looking at porn reveals an addiction (regardless of what you might tell yourself).

A problem with pornography will not just go away on its own.

Pornography is deceptive (pretends to be good while it is bad). It pleases; then it squeezes. It delights; then it bites. He that throws the boomerang of pornography in pleasure finds only that it *always* returns in pain.

> A problem with pornography will not just go away on its own.

Pornography portrays the fictitious as the real, not depict a normal sexual relation, but one "staged" and unnatural—a fantasy world.

Don't be naïve; there are people that feed on pornography whose intent is to lure others into its twisted and perverted web for their own purposes. In traveling on the Internet Highway, never let your guard down, lest you be victimized.

Don't *explore* (probe, search out, inspect) pornography. Paul wrote, "Make no provision for the flesh to arouse its desires" (Romans 13:14 NET). To explore it ("give place to it") not only is unnecessary but dangerous, for it gives place to erotic desires and urges. No one would drink rat poison to discover its deadly nature. They would simply read its warning label. It is likewise unnecessary to "explore" (get a taste of) pornography by viewing its content. Just read its "ingredients" label. To do otherwise (drink of its poisonous content) only serves "to arouse" the desires of the flesh for sexual misconduct.

Porn is not a harmless amusement. It leaves in its path pain, misery, sorrow, broken relationships, false expectations and a heart void of purity and wholesomeness.

Never concede defeat. It is a winnable battle. Many entangled in its twisted web have been set free through the liberating power of the Lord Jesus Christ. See John 8:36. Charles Dickens is correct: "We forge [make] the chains we bear in life."[114] Looking at pornography *binds* people with its chains (holds them captive to its control). It is a sobering thought that man doesn't possess in himself the necessary power to break its chains (position, popularity, prosperity are futile in the battle of the mind). But God does and can—and will!

He breaks the power of canceled sin;
    He sets the prisoner free.
His blood can make the foulest clean;
    His blood availed for me. ~ Charles Wesley (1739)

Oswald Chambers said, "Our battles are first won or lost in the secret places of our will in God's presence, never in full view of the world. The Spirit of God seizes me, and I am compelled to get alone with God and fight the battle before Him. Until I do this, I will lose every time. The battle may take one minute or one year, but that will depend on me, not God. However long it takes, I must wrestle with it alone before God, and I must resolve to go through the hell of renunciation or rejection before Him. Nothing has any power over someone who has fought the battle before God and won there."[115]

Allow remorse for the sin (porn) to work repentance in the soul (change of mind about ever doing it again), for such results in forgiveness and freedom through Jesus Christ. See 2 Corinthians 7:10 and 1 John 1:9.

The spiritual and physical *fast* is a means to tap hold of the power of God to break the yoke of porn. See Isaiah 58:6.

To be freed from the porn habit, a new habit must be inserted in its place, which the Lord will enable. Exert discipline with the new habit one day at a time, and gradually the tug of the old one will stop. In addition, solicit a friend or minister to be an accountability partner. See Galatians 6:2.

The battle to maintain purity will never end. To the unsuspecting, victory today may be followed by defeat tomorrow. Keep your heart fortified.

To stay free from pornography, wear the "Gospel Armor" (apply its truths) daily.

Accidents on the internet happen (things are seen unintentionally). At times you may see an erotic picture pop up while browsing. Exit the site at once, and you need not feel guilty. You can't stop a bird from landing on your head, but you can stop it from building a nest.

Don't let pornography make you afraid, just cautious and careful. It's like a tiger in a cage at the zoo. As long as the cage to porn is not opened or entered, it is harmless (to you).

The bottom line to freedom from and continuous victory over porn is spiritual focus. Set your focus on Christ and that which is holy. Paul admonishes: "Finally, believers, whatever is true, whatever is honorable and worthy of respect, whatever is right and confirmed by God's word, whatever is pure and wholesome, whatever is lovely and brings peace, whatever is admirable and of good repute; if there is any excellence, if there is anything worthy of praise, think continually on these things [center your mind on them, and implant them in your heart]" (Philippians 4:8 AMP).

10

To Change Means to Choose to Change

"For the weapons of our warfare are not carnal, but mighty through God to the pulling down of strong holds; Casting down imaginations, and every high thing that exalteth itself against the knowledge of God, and bringing into captivity every thought to the obedience of Christ" (2 Corinthians 10:4–5).

"Who we are today is the result of choices we made yesterday. Tomorrow, we will become what we choose today. To change means to choose to change."[116] ~ John Maxwell

> To change means to choose to change.—John Maxwell

Jesus asked a crippled man an odd question on the surface: "Do you want to get well?" (John 5:6 NIV). Why? It may have been that he had suffered in that condition so long, he was afraid he couldn't get well. If so, he is a lot like many hooked on (addicted, chained to) pornography. Having tried to get "well" without success (succeeding, victory), they have lost hope that it is possible.

Looking at pornography and continually feeding on it is a choice. You don't have to remain "crippled" (controlled and hurt by it). Jesus said, 'He that the son sets free, is free indeed' (John 8:36). Peter says, "The Lord knows how to deliver the godly out of temptations" (2 Peter 2:9 NKJV). John Wesley said, "It plainly appears from these instances [Noah; Lot], that the Lord knoweth, hath both wisdom and power and will, to deliver the godly out of all temptations."[117] No believer is exempt from temptation, *but* all may be unscathed by it through reliance upon the Lord. See 1 Corinthians 10:13.

Christ has set people free from porn for hundreds of years. When you are ready, He will to do the same for you.

> No believer is exempt from temptation, but all may be unscathed by it through reliance upon the Lord.

The Royal Ambassador pledge that I memorized as a young man is worthy to be heeded by all. In part it says,

"As a Royal Ambassador, I will do my best:

To keep myself clean and healthy, in mind and body."

Make that the motto of life, and it will spare you much grief and hurt. As a reminder to be cautiously selective of the internet websites you visit, post the pledge on the computers and iPads you utilize.

Honestly (with all your heart) make a solemn pact (agreement/decision) with God concerning avoiding pornography (total abstinence). It will be helpful to share the decision with another (parent, pastor, children's/youth minister, best buddy) for accountability and assistance in keeping it. Sign and have that person sign (witness) the following decision card:

MY SOLEMN PACT WITH GOD

'I made a solemn pact [agreement] with my eyes' (Job 31:1).

Today I make the decision not to look at or listen to anything that is pornographic and to keep myself pure and clean in mind and body.

Sign _____ Date _____

Witness _____ Date _____

It is most fitting to close this volume with an admonition from the apostle Paul:

"Why all this stress on behavior? Because, as I think you have realized, the present time is of the highest importance—it is time to wake up to reality. Every day brings God's salvation nearer. The night is nearly over, the day has almost dawned. Let us therefore fling away the things that men do in the dark, let us arm ourselves for the fight of the day! Let us live cleanly, as in the daylight, not in the 'delights' of getting drunk or playing with sex, nor yet in quarrelling or jealousies. *Let us be Christ's men from head to foot, and give no chances to the flesh to have its fling*" (Romans 13:11-14 PHILLIPS). Amen and Amen.

[1] McDowell, Josh, cited by Anugrah Kumar. "Josh McDowell Launches Website to Fight Porn, 'Church's No. 1 Threat'" (Christian Post, May 26, 2012).

[2] Jones, E. Stanley. *Abundant Living*. (Nashville: Abingdon-Cokesbury Press, 1942), 130.

[3] Spurgeon, C. H. "A Triumphal Entrance" (Sermon # 750), December 13, 1866.

[4] Rogers, Adrian. "The Poison of Pornography." https://www.oneplace.com/ministries/love-worth-finding/read/articles/the-poison-of-pornography-15292.html, accessed March 16, 2019.

[5] Fagan, Patrick. "The Escalation of Pornography: A Ten-Year Update, March 9, 2018. https://www.mercatornet.com/family_edge/view/the-escalation-of-pornography-a-ten-year-update/21116, accessed March 30, 2019.

[6] A recent study jointly commissioned by Covenant Eyes, Josh McDowell Ministry, and the Barna Group. http://christiannewsjournal.com/porn-use-rapidly-escalating-among-teens/, accessed March 30, 2019.

[7] Fagan, Patrick. "The Escalation of Pornography: A Ten-Year Update, March 9, 2018. https://www.mercatornet.com/family_edge/view/the-escalation-of-pornography-a-ten-year-update/21116, accessed March 30, 2019.

[8] Alvarez, Manny. "Porn Addiction: Why Americans Are in More Danger Than Ever", Fox News, March 30, 2019.

[9] Barna Group Survey, 2016, cited by Luke Gibbons. "15 Mind-Blowing Statistics About Pornography and the Church." https://conquerseries.com/15-mind-blowing-statistics-about-pornography-and-the-church/, accessed March 20, 2019.

[10] ibid.

[11] Huerta, Danny. "How Pornography Affects a Teen Brain." https://www.focusonthefamily.com/parenting/sexuality/kids-and-pornography/how-pornography-affects-a-teen-brain, accessed March 21, 2019.

[12] Pornography Statistics. www.familysafemedia.com/pornography_statistics.html, accessed October 17, 2011.

[13] Internet Statistics. https://www.guardchild.com/statistics/, accessed February 21, 2019.

[14] Challies, Tim. "10 Ugly Numbers Describing Pornography Use in 2017." April 11, 2017. https://www.challies.com/articles/10-ugly-and-updated-numbers-about-pornography-use/, accessed February 26, 2019.

[15] Ibid.

[16] Ibid.

[17] Josh McDowell. "The Porn Phenomenon: The Impact of Pornography in the Digital Age," 2016. p. 18. https://www.cbcrh.com/home/180005292/

180009741/docs/The-Porn-Phenomenon.pdf?sec_id=180009741, accessed March 8, 2019.
[18] Murphy, E. F. *Handbook for Spiritual Warfare*. (Nashville: Thomas Nelson, 1996), 122.
[19] Jackson, Rob. "When Children View Pornography." https://www.focusonthefamily.com/lifechallenges/love-and-sex/how-to-confront-children-using-pornography, accessed January 29, 2019.
[20] Internet Statistics. https://www.guardchild.com/statistics/, accessed February 21, 2019.
[21] ibid.
[22] Challies, Tim. "10 Ugly Numbers Describing Pornography Use in 2017." April 11, 2017. https://www.challies.com/articles/10-ugly-and-updated-numbers-about-pornography-use/, accessed February 26, 2019.
[23] https://www.statisticbrain.com/adult-film-industry-statistics-demographic.
[24] Internet Statistics. https://www.guardchild.com/statistics/, accessed February 21, 2019.
[25] Huerta, Danny. "How Pornography Affects a Teen Brain." https://www.focusonthefamily.com/parenting/sexuality/kids-and-pornography/how-pornography-affects-a-teen-brain, accessed March 21, 2019.
[26] Internet Statistics. https://www.guardchild.com/statistics/, accessed February 21, 2019.
[27] Hosley, Ryan and Steve Watters. "Dangers and Disappointments of Pornography." http://www.budapestresources.com/content/dangers-and-disappointments-of-pornography, accessed February 21, 2019.
[28] Ibid.
[29] MacArthur, John. "What is Truth?" August 4, 2009 (A379), https://www.gty.org/library/articles/A379/what-is-truth, accessed March 22, 2019.
[30] *Baker's Evangelical Dictionary of Biblical Theology*—Purity.
[31] Exell, Joseph. *The Biblical Illustrator,* Vol. 11 (Grand Rapids: Baker Book House, undated), 56.
[32] Staton, Knofel. *Check Your Character*. (New Life Books, 1981), 80–81.
[33] Huerta, Danny. "How Pornography Affects a Teen Brain." https://www.focusonthefamily.com/parenting/sexuality/kids-and-pornography/how-pornography-affects-a-teen-brain, accessed March 21, 2019.
[34] Cline, Victor B. "Pornography's Effect on Adults and Children." https://www.catholicnewsagency.com/resources/life-and-family/pornography/pornographys-effects-on-adults-and-children, accessed February 21, 2019.
[35] Rogers, Adrian. The Poison of Pornography, https://www.oneplace.com/ministries/love-worth-finding/read/articles/the-poison-of-pornography-15292.html, accessed March 16, 2019.

Endnotes

[36] Miner, Brad. "Satan Loves Porn." June 25, 2018. https://www.thecatholicthing.org/2018/06/25/satan-loves-porn/, accessed April 2, 2019.

[37] Graham, Billy. "Is There Anything Wrong With Pornography?" Tribune Content Agency on Apr 27, 2016. https://www.arcamax.com/healthandspirit/religion/billygraham/s-1816185, accessed February 9, 2019.

[38] Green, Tim. "Helps of Holiness" (Sermon). *Sword of the Lord*, December 28, 2018. (Murfreesboro: Sword of the Lord Publishers, 2018), 6.

[39] Drakeford, John and Jack Hamm. *Pornography: The Sexual Mirage.* (Nashville: Thomas Nelson, 1973), 160.

[40] Spurgeon, C. H. *Morning and Evening,* February 9 (Evening).

[41] Murphy, E. F. (1996). Handbook for spiritual warfare (p. 124). Nashville: Thomas Nelson.

[42] Meyer, F. B. cited in www.preceptaustin.org/james, James 1:13–15 Commentary, accessed October 13, 2011.

[43] Cline, Victor B. "Pornography's Effect on Adults and Children." https://www.catholicnewsagency.com/resources/life-and-family/pornography/pornographys-effects-on-adults-and-children, accessed February 21, 2019.

[44] Murphy, E. F. *Handbook for Spiritual Warfare.* (Nashville: Thomas Nelson, 1996), 125.

[45] Spurgeon, C. H. *Metropolitan Tabernacle Pulpit.* "Particular Redemption," February 28, 1858.

[46] Bonhoeffer, Dietrich, cited in Lust Quotes, christian-quotes.ochristian.com, accessed November 17, 2011.

[47] Love, T., C. Laier, M. Brand, L. Hatch, & R. Hajela. "Neuroscience of Internet Pornography Addiction: A Review and Update." (*Behavioral Sciences,* 5(3), 2015), 388–433. Doi: 10.3390/Bs5030388.

[48] Negash, S., N. Van Ness Sheppard, N. M. Lambert, & F. D. Fincham. "Trading Later Rewards for Current Pleasure: Pornography Consumption and Delay Discounting." (*The Journal of Sex Research,* 53(6), 2016), 698–700. Doi:10.1080/00224499.2015.1025123;
Voon, V., et al. "Neural Correlates of Sexual Cue Reactivity in Individuals with and without Compulsive Sexual Behaviors". (*PLoS ONE,* 9(7), 2014), E102419. Doi:10.1371/Journal.Pone.0102419;
Pitchers, K. K., et al. "Natural and Drug Rewards Act on Common Neural Plasticity Mechanisms with DeltaFosB as a Key Mediator." (*Journal of Neuroscience,* 33(8), 2013), 3434–3442. Doi:10.1523/JNEUROSCI.4881-12.2013

[49] "How Porn Changes the Brain," August 23, 2017. https://fightthenewdrug.org/how-porn-changes-the-brain/, accessed March 11, 2019.

[50] ibid.

[51] Volkow, N. D., G. F. Koob, & A. T. McLellan. "Neurobiological Advances from the Brain Disease Model of Addiction. (*New England Journal of Medicine,* 374, 2016), 363–371. Doi:10.1056/NEJMra1511480;
Pace, S. "Acquiring Tastes Through Online Activity: Neuroplasticity and the Flow Experiences of Web Users." (*M/C Journal,* 17(1), 2014). Retrieved from Http://Journal.Media-Culture.Org.Au/Index.Php/Mcjournal/Article/View/773

[52] Read Morton Montoya, "A Brief Introduction to the Damaging Effects of Porn on the Brain," for an explanation as to how the chemical actually works. The article, though technical, makes clear its effect on the brain. https://medium.com/metabolic-brain-disorders-ucsd/nsfnw-not-safe-for-neural-work-bfa50ddd422b, accessed March 29, 2019.

[53] "How Porn Changes the Brain," August 23, 2017. https://fightthenewdrug.org/how-porn-changes-the-brain/, accessed March 11, 2019.

[54] Volkow, N. D., G. F. Koob, & A. T. McLellan. "Neurobiological Advances from the Brain Disease Model of Addiction. (*New England Journal of Medicine,* 374, 2016), 363–371. Doi:10.1056/NEJMra1511480;
Sturman, D., & B. Moghaddam. "Reduced Neuronal Inhibition and Coordination of Adolescent Prefrontal Cortex During Motivated Behavior." (*The Journal of Neuroscience,* 31(4), 2011), 1471–1478. Doi:10.1523/JNEUROSCI.4210-10.2011;
Ehrlich, M. E., J. Sommer, E. Canas, & E. M. Unterwald. Periadolescent Mice Show Enhanced DeltaFosB Upregulation in Response to Cocaine and Amphetamine. (*The Journal of Neuroscience,* 22(21), 2002), 9155–9159. Retrieved from Http://Www.Jneurosci.Org/Content/22/21/9155

[55] Love, T., C. Laier, M. Brand, L. Hatch, & R. Hajela. "Neuroscience of Internet Pornography Addiction: A Review and Update." (*Behavioral Sciences,* 5(3), 2015), 388–433. Doi: 10.3390/Bs5030388.

[56] Volkow, N. D., & M. Morales. "The Brain on Drugs: From Reward to Addiction (*Cell,* 162(8), 2015), 713. Doi:10.1016/J.Cell.2015.07.046;
Nestler, E. J. "Transcriptional Mechanisms of Drug Addiction." (*Clinical Psychopharmacology and Neuroscience,* 10(3), 2012), 136–143. Doi:10.9758/Cpn.2012.10.3.136;
Hyman, S. E. "Addiction: A Disease of Learning and Memory." (*American Journal of Psychiatry,* 162(8), 2005), 1414–1422.

[57] Negash, S., N. Van Ness Sheppard, N. M. Lambert, & F. D. Fincham. "Trading Later Rewards for Current Pleasure: Pornography Consumption and Delay Discounting." (*The Journal of Sex Research,* 53(6), 2016), 698–700. Doi:10.1080/00224499.2015.1025123;

Endnotes

Hilton, D. L., & C. Watts. "Commentary On: Neuroscience Research Fails to Support Claims That Excessive Pornography Consumption Causes Brain Damage." (*Surgical Neurological International,* 2, 2011), 64. Doi:10.4103/2152-7806.81427;

Nestler, E. J. "Transcriptional Mechanisms of Addiction: Role of DeltaFosB." (*Philosophical Transactions of the Royal Society B: Biological Sciences,* 363(1507), 2008), 3245–3255. Doi:10.1098/Rstb.2008.0067.

[58] Cited in *National Publications: Young Salvationist,* www.salvationarmyusa.org. accessed November 18, 2011.

[59] "Pure Intimacy. The Effects of Prior Pornography Use on Marriage," www.pureintimacy.org/piArticles/A000000490.cfm, accessed November 21, 2011.

[60] Drakeford and Hamm. *Pornography: The Sexual Mirage.* (Nashville: Thomas Nelson, 1973), 145.

[61] A study by Utah State University.

[62] Huerta, Danny. "How Pornography Affects a Teen Brain." https://www.focusonthefamily.com/parenting/sexuality/kids-and-pornography/how-pornography-affects-a-teen-brain, accessed March 21, 2019.

[63] Challies, Tim. "10 Ugly Numbers Describing Pornography Use in 2017." April 11, 2017. https://www.challies.com/articles/10-ugly-and-updated-numbers-about-pornography-use/, accessed February 26, 2019.

[64] Drakeford, John W. and Jack Hamm. *Pornography: The Sexual Mirage.* (Nashville: Thomas Nelson, 1973), 145.

[65] Barna Group Survey, 2016 cited by Luke Gibbons. 15 Mind-Blowing Statistics About Pornography And The Church. https://conquerseries.com/15-mind-blowing-statistics-about-pornography-and-the-church/, accessed March 20, 2019.

[66] Manny Alvarez. Porn addiction: Why Americans are in more danger than ever, Fox News, March 30, 2019.

[67] Haverluck, Michael F. (OneNewsNow.com), Sunday, May 14, 2017. https://onenewsnow.com/church/2017/05/14/raped-at-6-josh-mcdowell-protect-kids-from-porn-at-5, accessed September 28, 2019.

[68] John Piper. "Battling the Unbelief of Lust," November 13, 1988. https://www.desiringgod.org/messages/battling-the-unbelief-of-lust, accessed March 6, 2019.

[69] Buechner, Frederick. *Godric,* (New York: Harpers Collins Publishers, 1980), 153.

[70] Thinkexist.com, accessed November 26, 2011.

[71] Huerta, Danny. "How Pornography Affects a Teen Brain." https://www.focusonthefamily.com/parenting/sexuality/kids-and-pornography/how-pornography-affects-a-teen-brain, accessed March 21, 2019.

[72] ibid.
[73] Covenant Eyes. https://www.covenanteyes.com/2014/10/03/7-necessary-tactics-beat-porn-addiction/, accessed March 20, 2019.
[74] Huerta, Danny. "How Pornography Affects a Teen Brain." https://www.focusonthefamily.com/parenting/sexuality/kids-and-pornography/how-pornography-affects-a-teen-brain, accessed March 21, 2019.
[75] Clarkson, William. "Spiritual Bondage and Christian Freedom" (sermon). https://biblehub.com/sermons/auth/clarkson/spiritual_bondage_and_christian_freedom.htm, accessed March 4, 2019.
[76] Love, T., C. Laier, M. Brand, L. Hatch, & R. Hajela. "Neuroscience of Internet Pornography Addiction: A Review and Update." (*Behavioral Sciences,* 5(3), 2015), 388–433. Doi: 10.3390/Bs5030388.
[77] Park, B. Y., et al. "Is Internet Pornography Causing Sexual Dysfunctions? A Review With Clinical Reports." (*Behavioral Sciences,* 6, 2016), 17. Doi:10.3390/Bs6030017;
Negash, S., N. Van Ness Sheppard, N. M. Lambert, & F. D. Fincham. "Trading Later Rewards for Current Pleasure: Pornography Consumption and Delay Discounting." (*The Journal of Sex Research,* 53(6), 2016), 698–700. Doi:10.1080/00224499.2015.1025123.
[78] Challies, Tim. "10 Ugly Numbers Describing Pornography Use in 2017." April 11, 2017. https://www.challies.com/articles/10-ugly-and-updated-numbers-about-pornography-use/, accessed February 26, 2019.
[79] Cline, Victor B. "Pornography's Effect on Adults and Children." https://www.catholicnewsagency.com/resources/life-and-family/pornography/pornographys-effects-on-adults-and-children, accessed February 21, 2019.
[80] Rogers, Adrian. "The Poison of Pornography." https://www.oneplace.com/ministries/love-worth-finding/read/articles/the-poison-of-pornography-15292.html, accessed March 16, 2019.
[81] Dobson, James. http://www.hitchedmag.com/print.php?id=134
[82] Doidge, N. *The Brain That Changes Itself.* (New York: Penguin Books, 2007), 208–212.
[83] C. J. Mahaney and Greg Someville. Why Small Groups? Together Toward Maturity (Gaithersburg, MD (Sovereign Grace Ministries, 1996), 6.
[84] Piper, John. *Future Grace*, Revised Edition. (Colorado Springs: Multnomah Books, 2012), 336.
[85] "Navigating Porn Addiction—A Guide for Parents." Therapy Associates, St. George, Utah, 2013.
[86] Stott, John. Langham Partnership Daily Thought, September 28, 2019. (Authentic Christianity, 1995).

[87] Nee, Watchman. "The Holy Word for Morning Revival." Hymn #767, (Week Three).
[88] Rogers, Adrian. "The Poison of Pornography." https://www.oneplace.com/ministries/love-worth-finding/read/articles/the-poison-of-pornography-15292.html, accessed March 16, 2019.
[89] Khoddam, Rubin. "5 Easy Tools to Resist the Urge of Bad Habits" (Nov 10, 2015). https://www.psychologytoday.com/us/blog/the-addiction-connection/201511/5-easy-tools-resist-the-urge-bad-habits, accessed January 29, 2019.
[90] Evans, Tony. "Overcoming Temptation." http://tonyevans.org/overcoming-temptation/, accessed December 7, 2017.
[91] Rogers, Adrian. "The Poison of Pornography." https://www.oneplace.com/ministries/love-worth-finding/read/articles/the-poison-of-pornography-15292.html, accessed March 16, 2019.
[92] *Expositor's Bible Commentary,* Psalm 40:2.
[93] *Merriam-Webster* and Literaryterms.net, accessed March 6, 2019.
[94] Lewis, C. S. *The Great Divorce.* (New York: Harper-Collins Publishers, 1946), 108–109.
[95] ibid., 111.
[96] ibid.
[97] ibid., 114.
[98] ibid., 39.
[99] https://www.azquotes.com/author/18200-Watchman_Nee, accessed March 4, 2019.
[100] Swindoll, Chuck. *Stress Fractures.* (Grand Rapids: Zondervan, 1995), 113.
[101] Radmacher, E. D., R. B. Allen, & H. W. House. *The Nelson Study Bible: New King James Version.* (Nashville: T. Nelson Publishers, 1997), Eph. 6:14.
[102] Henry, M. *Matthew Henry's Commentary on the Whole Bible: Complete and Unabridged in One Volume.* (Peabody: Hendrickson, 1994), 2319.
[103] Courson, J. *Jon Courson's Application Commentary.* (Nashville: Thomas Nelson, 2003), 1264.
[104] ibid.
[105] "The Great Teachings of the Bible and What They Mean for You: The Armor of God: Series 3." http://www.freebiblestudyguides.org/bible-teachings/armor-of-god-belt-of-truth.htm, accessed February 23, 2019.
[106] Anderson, Neil. *Victory Over the Darkness.* (Grand Rapids: Bethany House, 2014), 148.
[107] Henry, M. *Matthew Henry's Commentary on the Whole Bible: Complete and Unabridged in One Volume.* (Peabody: Hendrickson, 1994), 2319.
[108] ibid.

[109] https://www.christianquotes.info/quotes-by-topic/quotes-about-freedom/#ixzz5hCPxixcn, accessed March 4, 2019.
[110] Henry, M. *Matthew Henry's Commentary on the Whole Bible: Complete and Unabridged in One Volume.* (Peabody: Hendrickson, 1994), 2319.
[111] Courson, J. *Jon Courson's Application Commentary.* (Nashville: Thomas Nelson, 2003), 1264.
[112] Spurgeon, C. H. *Faith's Checkbook,* November 10.
[113] Anderson, Neil. *The Essential Guide to Spiritual Warfare.* (Grand Rapids: Bethany House, 2016), 70.
[114] braineyquote.com, accessed April 7, 2015.
[115] Chambers, Oswald. *My Utmost for His Highest,* December 27.
[116] Freeman-Smith. *Five Minutes of Peace.* (New York: Howard Books, 2009), 106.
[117] Wesley, John. *John Wesley's Explanatory Notes on the Whole Bible,* 2 Peter 2:9.

www.ingramcontent.com/pod-product-compliance
Lightning Source LLC
LaVergne TN
LVHW091319080426
835510LV00007B/555